Literacy Consultants
DAVID BOOTH • KATHLEEN GOULD LUNDY

Social Studies Consultant
PETER PAPPAS

A Harcourt Achieve Imprint

10801 N. Mopac Expressway
Building # 3
Austin, TX 78759
1.800.531.5015

Steck-Vaughn is a trademark of Harcourt Achieve Inc. registered in the United States of America and/or other jurisdictions. All inquiries should be mailed to: Paralegal Department, 6277 Sea Harbor Drive, Orlando, FL 32887.

Rubicon © 2007 Rubicon Publishing Inc.
www. rubiconpublishing.com

Project Editor: Kim Koh
Editor: Vicki Low
Editorial Assistants: Caitlin Drake, Joyce Thian
Art Director: Jen Harvey
Project Designer: Jan-John Rivera
Graphic Designer: Dana Delle Cese-Ahluwalia

7 8 9 10 11   5 4 3 2 1

Elephant Army
ISBN 13: 978-1-4190-3200-4
ISBN 10:   1-4190-3200-3

Printed in Singapore

PHOTO CREDITS: Shutterstock: 4-5, 13, 21, 29, 37, 45, 46-47; The Granger Collection, New York: 13, 21, 29, 46

Written by

SUZANNE MUIR

Illustrated by

ANTHONY BRENNAN

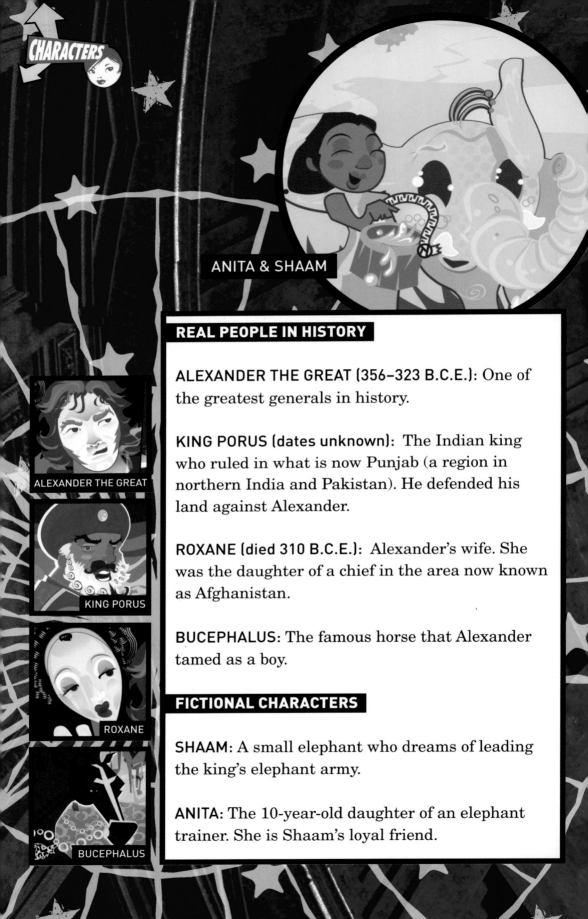

ANITA & SHAAM

REAL PEOPLE IN HISTORY

ALEXANDER THE GREAT

KING PORUS

ROXANE

BUCEPHALUS

ALEXANDER THE GREAT (356–323 B.C.E.): One of the greatest generals in history.

KING PORUS (dates unknown): The Indian king who ruled in what is now Punjab (a region in northern India and Pakistan). He defended his land against Alexander.

ROXANE (died 310 B.C.E.): Alexander's wife. She was the daughter of a chief in the area now known as Afghanistan.

BUCEPHALUS: The famous horse that Alexander tamed as a boy.

FICTIONAL CHARACTERS

SHAAM: A small elephant who dreams of leading the king's elephant army.

ANITA: The 10-year-old daughter of an elephant trainer. She is Shaam's loyal friend.

Contents

In the 4th century B.C.E., there was a mountainous kingdom called Macedonia, located just north of Greece. The Macedonians followed Greek culture, even though the Greeks were their enemies.

Macedonia was a powerful empire, especially under King Philip II and his son, Alexander. Alexander became king in 336 B.C.E., and would become one of the greatest military commanders of all time.

Alexander defeated the Persian Empire at the age of 25. He then set his eyes on India, the next prize.

The Indian king, Porus, knew Alexander was coming, and was prepared for the invading Macedonian army. He was ready with 2,000 cavalry, 20,000 infantry, and a secret weapon … elephants!

TIMELINE

356 B.C.E. »	344 B.C.E. »	343 B.C.E. »	336 B.C.E. »	334 B.C.E. »
Alexander is born in Pella, the capital of Macedonia.	According to legend, Alexander tames a wild black horse at age 12.	From age 13 to 16, Alexander is taught by the famous philosopher Aristotle.	Alexander becomes king of Macedonia when his father dies.	Alexander sets out with his army to conquer Persia.

WHAT'S THE STORY?

This story is set in an actual time in history and depicts real people, but some of the characters and events are fictitious.

333 B.C.E.	327 B.C.E.	326 B.C.E.	323 B.C.E.	321–315 B.C.E.
Alexander defeats Darius, the king of Persia.	Alexander marries Roxane. He begins his march to India.	Alexander fights against King Porus in the Battle of Hydaspes.	Alexander dies in Babylon.	King Porus is assassinated in this period.

CHAPTER 1: ALEXANDER ARRIVES

326 B.C.E.: ALEXANDER THE GREAT LEADS HIS ARMY THROUGH THE MOUNTAINS OF THE HIMALAYAS. THEY CROSS THE FAMOUS KHYBER PASS.

WILD STALLION

Alexander had his favorite horse, Bucephalus, for almost 20 years. The bond between them was so strong that Alexander named a city after him — Bucephala.

Bucephalus was a wild horse that a merchant had brought to Alexander's father. He was magnificent, but no one could ride him.

Alexander was only 12 years old at the time. He noticed that Bucephalus was afraid of his own shadow. Alexander led him toward the sun so that his shadow was behind him. Bucephalus calmed down and allowed Alexander to climb on his back. Alexander managed to tame the wild horse.

Alexander's father was very impressed. He told his son, "You must find a kingdom worthy of your talents, for Macedonia is too small for you."

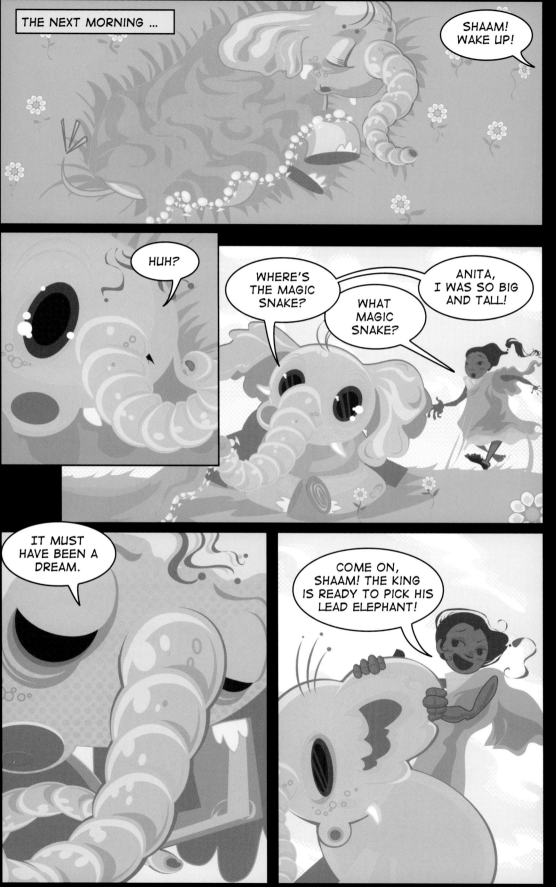

ALEXANDER DISCUSSES HIS PLAN OF ATTACK WITH THE GENERALS.
IF WE ATTACK ALL AT ONCE, WE WILL LOSE FOR SURE.
BUT WHAT DO YOU THINK WE SHOULD DO INSTEAD?
HERE'S MY PLAN ...
AHA! EXCELLENT!
I DON'T LIKE THIS AT ALL ...
LATER THAT NIGHT, ROXANE, ALEXANDER'S WIFE, TRIES TO TALK HIM OUT OF WAR.
ALEXANDER, I BEG YOU, CALL OFF THE ATTACK!
WHAT DO YOU MEAN? WE ARE POISED FOR VICTORY!
BUT THOSE ELEPHANTS! THEY WILL TERRIFY OUR HORSES AND OUR MEN.
NONSENSE!

WAR ELEPHANTS

People in Asia have been taming elephants for some 4,000 years. At first, elephants were used in farming, but from about 1,100 B.C.E. onward, they were used in war!

Generals used elephants to charge at the enemy. These war elephants could run at about 20 mph and were extremely strong and heavy. The enemy would either turn and flee or be trampled underfoot.

War elephants were first used in present-day India and Pakistan, but the practice spread to Egypt, Persia, and Carthage.

Elephant armies were very effective, but people soon came up with ways of fighting back. Julius Caesar, the famous Roman general, gave his men axes to chop at the elephants' legs. Other generals believed that elephants were afraid of pigs. They unleashed herds of pigs on the terrified elephants during battle!

THE GREEK WORLD

Greece was very advanced in Alexander's day. It was one of the world's leaders in philosophy, architecture, and the arts.

Aristotle teaching Alexander

ARISTOTLE (384 – 322 B.C.E.)

Aristotle was a philosopher, one of history's most famous thinkers. He was also Alexander's tutor. Aristotle started a very successful school in Athens, called the Lyceum. He is considered the father of today's scientific method or approach to knowledge.

The Parthenon

THE PARTHENON

The Parthenon is considered one of the finest monuments of ancient Greece. This magnificent temple was built in the 5th century B.C.E., but is still standing today. Many tourists visit the Parthenon to admire its impressive columns and decorative sculpture. It is one of the most visited sites in Greece today.

PAINTED POTTERY

In ancient Greece, artists created elegant pottery pieces. They often painted detailed scenes of heroes and gods directly onto the pottery. Because the ancient Greeks loved sports, they also painted sports scenes!

THE WAR ELEPHANTS CHARGE THE MACEDONIAN CAVALRY! SOLDIERS AND HORSES SCATTER.

KING PORUS FIGHTS FIERCELY, DEFENDING HIS COUNTRY WITH HIS SHINING SWORD!

GRRRR

THE MACEDONIANS FIGHT WITHOUT FEAR. UNDER ALEXANDER, THEY HAVE WON EVERY BATTLE!

ALEXANDER AND BUCEPHALUS CHARGE. PORUS IS KNOCKED OFF SHAAM'S BACK! AT THE SAME TIME, ALEXANDER IS HIT BY A SPEAR ...

ALEXANDER FALLS OFF BUCEPHALUS! NOW, BUCEPHALUS AND SHAAM FACE OFF ...

WITH A MIGHTY RUSH, SHAAM CATCHES BUCEPHALUS WITH HIS TUSKS AND THROWS HIM INTO THE AIR!

BASH!

BUCEPHALUS IS DEFEATED!

BUCEPHALUS, NOOO!

ANCIENT INDIA

On his way to the Hydaspes, Alexander had to cross the Indus — the river after which India is named. People have lived in the Indus Valley for at least 5,000 years.

At the time of Alexander's invasion, India was not one country but a number of small kingdoms. It was the center of a great civilization. It was also home to the religions of Hinduism and Buddhism.

Sanskrit was the language used in ancient India. Like Latin, Sanskrit has influenced other languages used today. Some of the greatest stories and poems ever written are in Sanskrit.

Statue of Buddha

Statue of the Hindu god Ganesha

SUDDENLY, ALEXANDER'S GENERAL CHARGES FROM THE SIDE! ALEXANDER HAS TRICKED PORUS AGAIN!

PORUS' WAR ELEPHANTS CANNOT HOLD THE LINE!

PORUS' ARMY IS DEFEATED. ALEXANDER ACCEPTS PORUS' OFFER OF SURRENDER.
YOU AND YOUR MEN FOUGHT WELL.
ALEXANDER, YOU HAVE WON THE BATTLE. I SURRENDER.
HOW DO YOU WISH TO BE TREATED, PORUS?
LIKE A KING.
VERY WELL. YOU SHALL CONTINUE TO RULE YOUR KINGDOM AS PART OF MY EMPIRE.
THANK YOU, MY LORD.

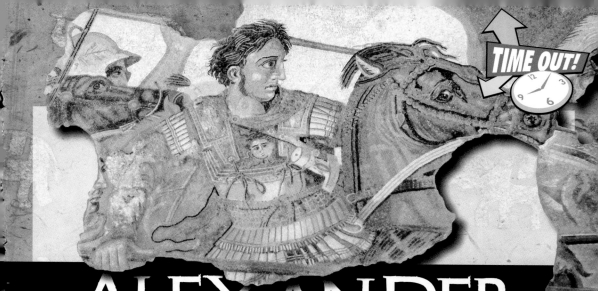

·ALEXANDER·
THE GREAT·

They didn't call him "Alexander the Great" for nothing!

Alexander created a vast empire. It spanned three continents: Europe, Africa, and Asia. The united empire was two million square miles, about half the size of Canada!

Alexander was a military genius. He never lost a single battle during his years of fighting. He perfected a military formation called the phalanx, where troops would stand close together, overlapping their shields and pointing their spears outwards.

Alexander was also a great leader. His troops were so devoted to him that they marched with him for 12 years, covering 10,600 miles of ground. They went through some of the world's most dangerous places, including mountain barriers, wild jungles, and dry deserts.

Phalanx formation

THE LEGEND LIVES ON

Alexander was only 32 when he died, but he had changed the world forever.

From Greece in the west to India in the east, from the river Danube in the north to Egypt in the south — all these lands were united in a single empire.

Millions of people came under his rule. These people spoke many different languages and followed various customs. Alexander accepted the cultures of the lands he conquered. He married a foreign princess, Roxane, and adopted many Persian habits.

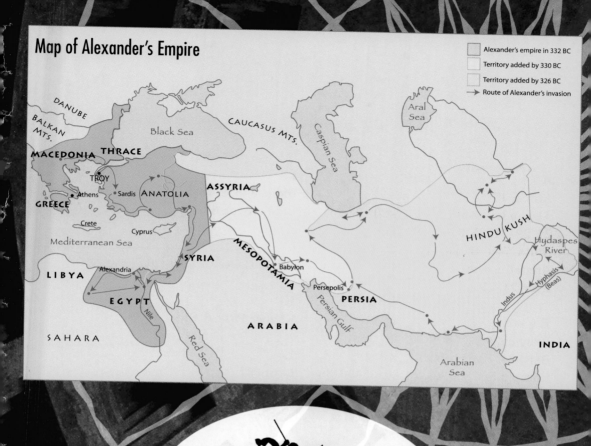

Map of Alexander's Empire

Alexander's empire in 332 BC
Territory added by 330 BC
Territory added by 326 BC
→ Route of Alexander's invasion

DANUBE

BALKAN MTS.

Black Sea

CAUCASUS MTS.

Aral Sea

Caspian Sea

MACEDONIA THRACE

GREECE

TROY

Athens • Sardis • ANATOLIA

ASSYRIA

HINDU KUSH

Hydaspes River

Crete

Cyprus

Mediterranean Sea

MESOPOTAMIA

SYRIA

Babylon

Indus

Hyphasis (Beas)

LIBYA

Alexandria

Persepolis

PERSIA

EGYPT

Nile

ARABIA

Persian Gulf

SAHARA

Red Sea

INDIA

Arabian Sea

Alexander's conquests were so impressive that he was worshipped as a god in Egypt. He was a gifted, ambitious man, but he was also cruel and ruthless. He has fascinated and inspired people through the ages. Julius Caesar and Napoleon were two of his greatest admirers. More than 2,300 years after his death, Alexander is still the subject of movies and books.

INDEX